Herman C Meadows, Jr.
1550 N. Golf Blvd
Columbia, MO 65202
e-mail: hcm@mchsi.com
Phone: 573-4748879
Cell Phone: 573-489-5545
Order on line: Barnes and Noble: Amazon.com

PROOF OF LOSS

A quick guide to processing insurance
claims for insured with their adjuster

HERMAN MEADOWS

iUniverse, Inc.
Bloomington

Proof of Loss
A quick guide to processing insurance claims for insured with their adjuster

iUniverse books may be ordered through booksellers or by contacting:

iUniverse
1663 Liberty Drive
Bloomington, IN 47403
www.iuniverse.com
1-800-Authors (1-800-288-4677)

ISBN: 978-1-4502-5838-8 (sc)
ISBN: 978-1-4502-5839-5 (ebook)

Printed in the United States of America

iUniverse rev. date: 6/03/2011

Table of Contents

Introduction

<u>The Purpose</u>

There are as many stories about what insurance adjusting is, how it works, who benefits and the purpose of adjusting as there are people who have been involved with an insurance claim.

My purpose for writing this book is three fold:

   📁 First, to provide information about the insurance adjusting profession to people who may be interested in pursuing the profession as a career.

   📄 Second, to provide information to the "insured" or "claimant" to enable them to understand more about insurance adjusting and how it works for them. At some time if they have a claim, they'll better understand what is involved. Each chapter will be on a different topic that relates to insurance or with the adjusting process. It will cover the entire process, from the time you purchase a policy or become involved in a claim or liability situation, to the time the loss or claim is concluded. I will share with you some interesting stories, some difficult situations and some emotional situations that I've encountered during my 40+ years as an adjuster.

   📄 Finally, I hope that anyone who reads this book will come

to understand that insurance adjusters are professional people who provide a service to others. This service is intended to help victims to recover from a situation that has caused them loss, hardship or temporary deviation from their normal living. This is the whole crust of why insurance is sold: to provide the policy holders with a monetary source to help them pay the costs of restoring their insured properties (or to recover from an unexpected loss that is covered by the policy).

About the Author

I was born in Shreveport, Louisiana on February 2, 1936. I graduated from high school in 1954, and attended Louisiana State University for 3 years. After changing majors two times (and flunking out twice), I finally received a degree in Business from Centenary College in Shreveport.

Following graduation in May 1960, I married my present wife Shirley. We raised 3 children. I sold life insurance for 3 years, and had a couple of jobs, but wasn't satisfied.

God has been a significant part of my life. He must have been looking after me, because a friend of mine and I were talking and he told me, "You can do better for yourself than what you are doing." He told me that the office of an insurance adjusting company was looking for inspectors to appraise damage in south Louisiana.

I went to the office, applied and got the job, and my adjusting career was born. That was in the year 1965. I began working claims for a major insurance adjustment company in January 1966 and more than 40 years have been spent in the insurance adjusting profession. I formally retired in May of 2006.

Chapter 1

Mrs. Smith is in the family room reading. Suddenly, the smell leads her to the kitchen, where she finds a skillet of cooking oil on fire. The room is rapidly filling with smoke. "Honey! Honey! Come quick, the kitchen stove is on fire!" Mr. Smith enters the room and, thinking quickly, picks up the phone and dials 911 to summon the fire department. Fortunately, the fire trucks are close by and they arrive in minutes, although it seems like hours to the Smiths.

In the interim, Mr. Smith has located the fire extinguisher and sprays the chemical on the skillet fire – wrong extinguisher, and the fire continues to burn! Thinking quickly, he pours flour on the fire and is able to put it out. Unfortunately, the house has filled with smoke.

The fire truck arrives, and the firefighters remove the skillet and hook up huge exhaust fans, which pull the smoke out of the house. (No small feat, considering the house has 8 rooms and a basement.)

Mr. Smith explains that he had put the skillet and oil on the stove, planning to fry fish and hush puppies for the evening. Unfortunately, he took a detour to his woodworking shop in the basement, started working on a loose end, and forgot about the pan on the stove. The firefighters complete their paperwork, and they tell the Smiths that a copy of the fire report will be available in 3 working days.

This is a small incident as claims go, but it involves many people and much interaction between:

📑 The insurance agent: The person representing the insurance company and sells the insurance product to best suit the client's need . The contact person between the client and the company when the client has a question or wants to make a change in his or her insurance program.

▯ The insurance company: The company that enters into a contractual agreement with the client to provide insurance coverage. The contract information contains coverage information and conditions related to the client's needs.

⧗ The insurance adjuster: The person representing the insurance company who works with the insured in handling the insured's claim.

⌨ The claims office: A department of the insurance company where claims are processed.

🖑 The contractors: People who work with the insured and adjuster to help evaluate damage in a claim situation

🖱 Field adjuster: Adjuster who goes to the location of the occurrence and works with the insured to obtain information relative to the claim .

A Claim is Born

The following chapters explain who is involved and what must take place to get the Smith's claim handled – and get the Smiths back to a normal environment. The adjuster is the person who coordinates most of these activities, and must do so in a prompt and professional manner.

Chapter 2

What Do We Do Now?

At some time prior to this fire, the Smiths saw an insurance agent and took out an insurance policy on their house. I would like for you, the reader, to take a moment and jot down the name of the agent who sold you your Homeowners policy and your Automobile policy. Can you do this without looking it up? Most people can name their agent – however, you would be surprised at the number of people who purchased insurance, locked the policy in a safe deposit box at their bank and no longer remember either their agent or even their insurance company!

Tip: Keep your agent and insurance company contact information handy.

The first thing that Mr. and Mrs. Smith should do is call their agent and inform the agent of the event. The agent will arrange to get the information from them and complete a loss nature form. He may do this by phone, or he may come to the insured's home so he can get an idea of the physical damage. Some agents give the insured the phone number of the claims office. The insured then calls the company claims office a reports the claim.

The agent will tell the Smiths what contact arrangement will probably be made for them to meet with an adjuster. Now the third party – the insurance company – becomes involved. The agent probably faxes or emails the loss notice to the claims department of the insurance company. The loss notice is sent to the claims supervisor, who reviews the loss and decides what office adjuster will coordinate the processing of the claim and conclusion.

There are still decisions to be made. Perhaps this is a small insurance company that lacks its own staff field adjuster, so the company calls on an independent insurance adjusting contractor to service claims. In such a case, an approved independent contractor is chosen and the claim assignment is sent to that adjusting company, who routes the information to the adjuster for that area.

It's very important that the adjuster contact the Smiths within 24 hours of receiving the assignment – the adjuster must arrange to meet them at the property for a first-hand look at the damage.

Naturally, the Smiths aren't sitting around doing nothing while these arrangements are being made! The two of them start cleaning the stove and surrounding area, and verify that no lasting damage has been done to the stove itself. The Smiths should also begin keeping a list of the items that need to be discussed with the adjuster, noting the areas throughout the house where smoke and soot have accumulated. The contents of the kitchen and adjoining rooms should be carefully examined as well. Finally, the Smiths take the time to write down any questions that they have concerning the adjustment process.

Chapter 3

Who Is This Stranger At My Door?

The adjuster arrives at the Smith residence, and introduces himself. Perhaps he gives them a business card and begins a pleasant conversation to help the Smiths relax. I have shown my card and a copy of the loss report, which carries their agent's name and the name of their insurance company.

The adjuster explains what needs to be accomplished on this first visit. This work may include:

📁📁	Taking photos of the damage.
📁📁	Drawing a diagram of the house.
📁📄	Taking the dimensions of each room.
📁📄	Creating a room-by-room list of damage.
📁📄	Creating a room-by-room list of the restoration work required.

Once these tasks are done, the adjuster sits down with the Smiths – or they move from room-to-room – and they all review the notes the adjuster has made. This is the time the insured individuals should ask the adjuster any questions regarding the work.

Tip: Ask questions whenever you're unsure of what's happening, or why!

This is a good time for the adjuster to evaluate how the communication with the insured is working: are they quiet and laid back, not asking many questions? Are the insured individuals open and responsive to the adjuster's questions and comments?

I always take a moment during this initial meeting to discuss with the insured the amounts of coverage applicable to each item that makes up the policy – then, it's time to discuss the cost of the necessary repairs required to get the home and its contents restored, cleaned or replaced. Typically, the adjuster leads the insured through the process of settling on a cost figure.

The adjuster may decide to return to the office and work on the estimate, then get back to the insured and go over the figures. If the insured is agreeable then the adjuster can submit the figures to the insurance company and request a fast payment, calling in a contractor if the damage is extensive enough.

Chapter 4

Insurance Explained

How many different insurance policies or coverage plans do you have? List them, and what your costs are, and you may be amazed at what you're paying for and how much of a bite your insurance takes out of your wallet or purse!

In this day and time, how many things do you identify by numbers? Your phone, address, and driver's license immediately come to mind, but what about your insurance? Most people don't think of a number when they consider their:

- homeowners policy
- auto coverage
- liability
- medical
- dental
- workman's compensation
- life insurance

Each type of insurance I just mentioned is sold to cover a need for specific protection, and the way you handle each type of coverage will vary during the adjusting process (due to the coverage and information needed to process a claim). The goal, however, is to provide the person with a fair and equitable conclusion in compliance with the policy they have in force, or the coverage they are exposed to because of an action on their part. Unfortunately, all damages or losses incurred in an event are not covered by the policy in force – we'll cover situations like these in later chapters.

An insurance policy is a binding contract between the insurer (the company issuing the policy) and the insured (the owner of the property or the person performing the activity being insured). The policy limits, coverage, deductible and exclusions are issued to accurately and adequately insure the described property or activity according to its needs. For this protection, the insurance company determines how much the insured should pay for the protection (as a premium).

The policy is usually issued for a period of 1, 2 or 3 years, with specific dates it remains in force, and a specific date of expiration. The policy outlines the coverage, conditions, exclusions and limit of coverage.

Many policies have a stated deductible. When a loss amount is determined, the deductible is subtracted and the net amount is called the claim amount and is paid by the insurance company.

The deductible amount on some policies is negotiable, and the premium is adjusted accordingly. The higher the deductible, the lower the premium. These options are worked out before the policy is issued, between the insurance company and the insured – the agent typically coordinates the process.

For example, your homeowners policy on your house likely has a number of limits built-in. They might include:

- Dwelling - $100,000
- Personal Property - $60,000
- Additional Living Expenses - $20,000

🗁/🗁   Deductible - $500

When a policy is issued and the premium paid, the insurance company and the insured are bound to the agreement outlined in the policy. Naturally, the insured's situation will change as time passes, and likewise insurance needs change as well.

Things change with the insured as life progresses… likewise, insurance needs change. The insured should sit down with his agent every couple of years and review his policy to see if any coverage needs to be added or deleted; for example, to see if there is enough dollar coverage on the insured items in case the insured suffers a total loss.

Most homeowner policies have an inflation clause, which automatically increases a certain amount each year. Adjusters are kept up to date of changes in policy provisions and changes by the companies they represent.

When the insured has a claim, the adjuster gets policy information that the company has on record at the time of the loss, and this is what the adjuster uses as a base for the policy coverage. The adjuster has to have a good knowledge of the coverage afforded on the policy in force on the property involved with the occurrence, including the items that are excluded from coverage within the policy.

For example, here are some common exclusions in property insurance:

🗁/📄   Intentional acts by the insured
🗁/📄   Normal wear and tear
🗁/📄   Trees damaged by wind
🗁/📄   Losses in excess of dollar limits stated in the policy

⌷⌛   Some types of water damage
⌷▦   Theft loss without evidence of forced entry

Co-insurance is an area that helps determine the amount of payment due the insured on a claim. On a homeowner policy, the company usually has an 80-90% co-insurance clause. This means that the property should be insured at least 80% of the replacement cost and get full payment of the claim. For example, if it costs $100,000 to rebuild a house at the time of the loss, the policy should have 80-90% insurance coverage, or $80,000-$90,000 in force. If the policy has $60,000 insurance on a $100,000 replacement cost, the claim is subject to a co-insurance penalty, and it will only pay 75% of the claim amount. Co-insurance is a good reason why the insured should go over the policy with the agent every year or two, to monitor changes in the value of the policy.

Chapter 5

So You Want to Become an Adjuster...

The insured today probably has need for several different insurance policies. The insurance industry has the need for several different types of adjusters. The major types of insurance coverage that rely on adjusters include:

Property (residential, commercial and business, including dwellings and their contents)

Auto (physical damage, collision/comprehensive/liability)

Liability (business and personal)

Marine (watercraft)

Adjusters are trained to handle claims in one or more of these types, as needed by the companies they represent. There are three major categories of professional adjuster:

1. Staff adjusters. These adjusters are employed by one company and handle claims for only that company.

2. Independent adjusters. Working for adjustment companies, these individuals represent many different insurance companies, most of whom do not have their own field adjusters.

3. Public adjusters. Adjusters hired by the insured to represent them regarding a specific claim with an insurance company.

In 42 years of claims handling I worked for many insurance companies. I owned my own claims service for 13 years. I was a multi-line adjuster all of my career (handling property, auto and liability claims in all three capacities).

A person thinking about becoming an adjuster will need a number of skills to succeed, including:

   📄📄 Good people skills, including communication with everyone involved in the insurance transaction... the insured, contractors, lawyers and insurance company staff, to name a few.

   📄📄 Patience, since adjusting often requires that you work at a pace that won't confuse the insured

   📄📄 Attention to details, including information requested by the insured that you'll have to work to find

   📄📄 And the most important characteristic you'll need... a good adjuster must be a good listener! You must give the insured the time to provide you with the complete details – after all, they're the reason you have a job, and the insured are often upset or angry, and usually know very little about the ins and outs of the claim procedure.

Pay and benefits have improved substantially over the past 10 to 15 years with insurance companies for their adjusting personnel. For example, in 1966 (when I started with an adjusting company in Lake Charles, Louisiana) I received $400 per month, a company car, and health insurance for myself and my family. During the late 70's, when I had my own adjusting business, I typically grossed $30,000 a year. By the mid-eighties, salaries, benefits, and medical coverage offered to employees by insurance companies were more favorable.

An adjuster starting out today with a major insurance company will have a decent income and retirement program to build on. However, the learning process for an adjuster is a long one, and the insurance company that hires a novice adjuster invests a lot of time and money in training. If a new adjuster likes the profession and stays with it, at least a year is required just to learn the bare necessities, and the learning process is ongoing. In fact, I've been learning for 41 years!

Chapter 6

Handling Mood Swings: The Insured & The Adjuster

Throughout life people come face to face with the unexpected. When it occurs, the person or people affected react – for example, three people faced with the same event may react 3 different ways, because each person is different.

Remember Mrs. Smith? She discovered a fire in a skillet on the stove. She probably panicked and yelled for help; in her case, Mr. Smith was home, and he came immediately, so they were able to handle the situation by calling the fire department, and then calling their insurance agent. In this case, when the adjuster arrives a day or two later, much of the clean up has been done, there's no major loss or damage and the Smiths are calm. The claim process goes smoothly.

But what if Mr. Smith had been at the store, buying something for the meal, when the fire occurred? If Mrs. Smith had been alone when she found the fire, what would her reaction have been? Or what if the Smiths had both gone to the store, forgetting about the skillet, run into some friends and stopped to chat? This time, when the Smiths return home, they see the fire department's trucks already there, and smoke and flame licking around the roof.

The Smiths reactions now are completely different. "Did you turn off the skillet before we left?" asks Mrs. Smith. (I won't publish his answer.) Now you have guilt, anger and uncertainty – and the Smiths have lost their home, all of its contents and treasured personal possessions, due to something that could have been avoided.

When the adjuster arrives to handle the claim, he finds a much different set of circumstances to deal with, including the emotions of the insured towards him and each other. The adjuster has to work with the insured to try to help them. He must communicate with them in a positive frame of mind, investigate the cause of the loss, establish the cost of the loss and get the insured to produce a personal property list. The property list includes

📄	The item name
📄	A description
📄	The age of the item
📄	Where the Smiths bought the item
📄	The original cost of the item
📄	The current replacement cost

The insured has an obligation under the insurance policy to provide the adjuster with the most accurate information they have relating to the personal property that's been lost – and don't forget, it may take the insured a couple of weeks just to produce the list. The insured individuals will likely have jobs, and they need to arrange for a place to stay while the house is repaired, as well as buy new clothing to replace the items damaged by smoke and fire.

It's always traumatic for the insured to return to what remains of each room of a burned home to prepare a list of the items that room once held. I have had situations where the insured actually has a family member who's familiar with the house and its contents prepare the list, which saves the insured the heartache of revisiting the damage. The insured later fills in the information and details for each item. However, most of us don't realize how much we carry in our heads until we have to recall the contents of an entire room, much less an entire home.

Therefore, my recommendation to the insured is that they take the time to make a list of each item in every room, the basement, the garage and the attic every couple of years, **before** such a disaster strikes – the list should provide as much of the information I listed above as possible. Renewing this list every 2 years or so should become a household tradition… that's because we buy furniture and appliances an average of 7 times during our lifetimes. Keep your agent informed of any extensive or expensive purchases or improvements that might require an increase in your insurance – a phone call or a quick stop by your agent's office may save the insured thousands of dollars in case of a disaster like the Smiths experienced!

The adjuster's moods may be similar to the insured's, but affected for different reasons:

- **Sadness.** It's easy to feel sadness for the loss that the insured have sustained.
- **Patience.** You must be able to listen to the insured when they need to express their feelings about the loss, which is very common while the adjuster is waiting for the insured to complete a list.
- **Anger.** An emotion never expressed to the insured. This is where an adjuster's "windshield" (or driving time) comes in. The adjusters realize that in many claims, the incident could have been avoided by some common sense on the part of the insured. (Mr. Smith, of course, would have been better off if that stove had been turned off before leaving the house. Perhaps Mr. Smith

even said to himself, "We'll be back from the store in 10 minutes." Anger can even lead to difficult times when gathering information from the insured.

🔲 **Joy.** I've experienced joy when settling some claims, after the insured have been paid and they're satisfied with the service they've received.

An adjuster must be prepared to deliver bad news as well. Perhaps the policy doesn't cover the loss, or the coverage is less than what's necessary to replace the insured's loss. The adjuster will likely have a copy of the exclusion to show the insured, but that often doesn't help the situation. I've encountered responses like these in the past:

🔲 "I was afraid that would be the case."
🔲 "My agent said I had full coverage."
🔲 "I was not aware of that provision."
🔲 "I know if you nullify the claim you'll get paid more by the insurance company."

Another situation can occur concerning the deductible. For example, suppose the adjuster and the insured reach an agreed adjustment on the loss totaling $897.52. The adjuster says, "Mr. Smith, I'm sorry, but the policy information shows you have a $1000 deductible. Therefore, no payment can be made on your loss." Now you must deal with an immediate and sudden hostility on the part of the insured... perhaps the insured says, "I'm certain that my deductible is only $500!" The insured scrambles to find his policy, certain that he is in the right... only to find a few minutes later that the coverage sheet on the policy does indeed show $1000 as the deductible. When the insurance company renewed Mr. Smith's policy, they changed the deductible from $500 to $1000, and attached a notice in writing on the policy jacket or at the end of the policy itself. Of course, the insured didn't notice this communication, concentrating only on the premium that was due.

I can't stress this point enough for anyone carrying insurance: **it is vitally important that you look over your policy each time it's renewed to see if any new information or changes have been included with the policy! If changes have been made and you're not comfortable with the result, contact your agent and express your concern.** (Naturally, your agent doesn't have time to contact all 10,000 of his clients to advise each of the change, so a written notice must suffice.)

Chapter 7

<u>Stories and Situations</u>

In this chapter, I'll present a few stories and situations that I think may illuminate some of the challenges and rewards of adjusting. Each one has taught me an important lesson in my effort to become a better adjuster. Enjoy!

1. About six months after I went to work in Lake Charles, Louisiana, I was sent out on a number of simple claims. I had attended adjusting school, studying basic policies covering homes. There had been a wind storm and two trees had been blown down. I anxiously jotted down the type of tree, age and measured the diameter of the tree. With this information, I went back to the office to discuss my activities with my manager.

   When my manager learned I was talking about a tree blown over by wind, he told me no policy covers such damage. There was a pause as I absorbed this information, then I realized I had to go back to the insured and explain why they had no coverage for the tree.

   Lesson Learned: Go over restrictions with your manager or co-adjuster if you're not sure of the

insured's coverage.

2. I had a claim with an elderly man at his farm. He had on old dirty coveralls, but he was polite and we got along very well. When I started to leave, he said, "Meadows, I enjoyed working with you. However, if we ever have a claim together again, please don't come on my property wearing a coat and tie!"

   I can only suspect at some time in the past, someone "dressed up" took him for some money or wronged him somehow, and all people "dressed up" were crooks!

   Lesson Learned: Stay sensitive to the mood and body language shown by the insured.

3. I had my own adjustment business in Hannibal, Missouri. My office was in a one room space in a building that had been a service station. An attorney had purchased it, converted it to his offices and rented out this one room. No windows, but at least it had a door!

   I had an unsatisfactory involvement with an insured, and he left angry. A couple of days later he called me and said, "I'm going to beat you up!" I hesitated, then replied, "You're going to have to do two things before you can hurt me."

   Of course, he demanded to know what these prerequisites were. In an even voice, I told him, "First you have to find me, then you have to catch me." Since he weighed over 250 pounds, I knew I could out-run him... and I never heard any more from him!

Lesson Learned: Don't lose your cool in the face of an angry insured.

4. A businessman that sold propane fuel went to a customer's farm to deliver some of the gas. While on the property and in the process of filling the propane tank, the customer's prize hunting dog got under the truck. When the tank was filled and the man started to leave, he ran over the dog and killed it. The customer wanted the man to pay him a whopping $300 for his dog.

   The gas customer reported the accident to his insurance agent. The claim was assigned to me, and I investigated. I thought, "$300 for a dog?" Since this was a potential liability claim, I focused on the fact that the businessman didn't do anything to lure or force the dog under the truck. The man had no idea the dog was under the truck, so the insured had no obligation to check under his vehicle.

   I made my report to the company and recommended that they deny the claim being made by the customer for his dog. The company did in fact deny the claim. Months later, I spoke to the businessman, who told me the customer hadn't purchased any more propane from him. (Not surprising, I think.)

   Lesson Learned: Check under your vehicle in those rural areas!

5. My final story is by far the most emotional story and experience of my entire 41 years in the claims profession.

In the fall of 1967 I was working a storm in Brownsville, Texas. Brownsville is located on the Texas-Mexico border, and at the time was almost half Mexican in population. The claim I was working involved a young family whose house had been damaged in the storm.

Most of the folks in the neighborhood did not have much, but what they had they were proud of – for example, houses were kept immaculately clean. I met with the lady of the house and she gave me a tour through the building, showing me places where the roof had leaked and the water had left stains on the ceiling and walls. Following us as we went from room to room were two of the family's small children. One was a two year old, while the other was four years old. The two year old was cute, outgoing and caught my eye. I bent down close to him and said, "You are a cute little fellow. For just a little bit, I could take you home with me."

The mother and I completed the list of things she knew that were damaged. I completed my work, told her the insurance company would be getting in touch with her, and went back to my car. I was sitting in the car looking at the information for my next stop, and the mother came up to the driver's side window and tapped the glass. Thinking she had a question about the claim, I rolled the window down and said, "Yes ma'am, can I help you?" In broken English, she replied, "Would you really like to take my baby home with you?" After a pause, I could say nothing but "Ma'am?" She repeated the question, saying, "We will not be able to provide him with the life that you and your family could."

I politely declined and left as soon as I could. It was about 1:30PM – I was so shook up that I returned to my hotel room and stayed there the rest of the day. My wife and I had three pre-school children in Rolla, Missouri at the time, and the day I was able to start back home did not come too soon.

I was 31 years old at the time, and have on many occasions since then remembered the love and willingness of this family to give up one of their flesh and blood so he could have a better life than they felt they could provide for him. What a sacrifice! I could not wait to see my wife and our children and hug them tightly.

Lesson Learned: Be prepared to be touched by your profession.

Chapter 8

Liability Insurance: The Insured, the Company, the Claimant

A liability arises when a person or persons cause an occurrence that results in injury and/or property damage to someone else, or a property belonging to someone else. The event causing the accident is one which would not have happened had the insured been paying attention to the situation just before the accident, and taken action to prevent the accident.

For example, you are driving a car and it becomes evident that an accident is going to happen – it's likely that the accident is over only 4 to 6 seconds from the beginning of the event. The result can range from very minor to catastrophic for those involved in the accident, and one or more claims may result.

Liability insurance is written to cover a specific operation, like a business, a city or a hospital. Liability insurance is designed to protect the insured operation in case an employee or someone related to the insured causes an accident, including physical damage to someone else's property or bodily injury to someone through a negligent act on the part of the person causing the accident.

Liability coverage can also be written as a section of coverage of a policy insuring specific things. For example, the homeowners policy on a residence will usually include coverage for physical damage to the dwelling and contents. Another section of the same policy relates to liability. Automotive coverage can be written the same way, with one section covering physical damage to the vehicle and another section of the same policy covering liability.

Some of the same people are involved in liability claims are also involved in the homeowner and automobile claims mentioned in earlier chapters, including:

    The insured

    The agent

    The insurance company itself

However, we can also add some other people who become a major part of the liability claim:

    The claimant

    The lawyer

    The doctor

    The police

    The claims expediter

The following pages will mention several parts of the liability coverage in the reader's policies, which will help you to better understand your policy and what the adjuster is talking about concerning dollars and claim settlements.

Liability coverage has two major categories:

1. **Property damage to others.** Some policies list a specific limit for property damage claims, such as $25,000 or $50,000 limits (depending on the insured's exposure to risk). This means the insurance would only be responsible for the stated limit in the policy> Say 25,000. If the insured caused $40,000 damage to someone's property, the insured would have to pay the amount over the $25,000 policy limit., in this case $15,000.

2. **Bodily injury to others.** Limits in this category are usually expressed with two figures, like $100,000/$300,000. The first number represents the limit per person, per occurrence. The second number represents the total limit per occurrence. For instance, multiple people may make injury claims because of an accident, but the maximum dollar amount to be paid out per event is $300,000. (Of course, these limits are determined by information obtained by the agent on the application completed by the prospective insured. The application is sent to the underwriting department for review, so the premium that the insured pays is determined in part by the amounts of coverage insured in the policy.)

Note that some insurance companies issue a combination limit for property damage and bodily injury under one limit.

Remember, the insurance policy is a two-party binding contract. The insured pays a premium to the insurance company in exchange for a policy that fits his needs.

In the following two chapters, I'll cover liability investigation and liability settlement.

Chapter 9

Investigation: Liability

Facts... who do they come from?

▦▤ **The insured driver, and the passengers in the insured vehicle.** Remember, the person sitting in the front seat may see the accident happen a little differently from the person sitting in the back seat.

▦▥ The driver of the other vehicle and the passengers acting as witnesses.

▦▦ Information developed from the police report.

▦▧ Information developed the emergency personnel who respond to the accident scene.

▦▨ **The accident reconstruction team.** These folks are usually with the police department, sheriff's department or state highway patrol.

Liability isn't always clear. In a two-vehicle accident, for example, one driver can be at fault or both drivers may be at fault. Some states now have statues in place outlining *Comparative Negligence*: both drivers are responsible for the accident, and through investigation, the percentage of fault that each driver is responsible for is established as accurately as possible. (The ratio might be 50%-50%, or 80%-20%.)

If the insured whom the adjuster represents is found to have the majority percentage at fault, then his company pays the other driver a corresponding percentage of the damage figure on her car, as well as the same percentage of the bodily injury settlement, if a bodily injury claim is made. For example, if the insured is found to be 80% at fault, then 80% of the damage figure is paid to the other driver, as well as 80% of the BI settlement (if one is made).

The insurance company representing the driver with the minority percentage – in this case, 20% – pays the insured 20% of the damage figure on the vehicle and 20% of the BI settlement (if any).

The adjuster involved coordinates the investigation process. The adjuster does as much as is necessary to develop an accurate account of the facts to establish liability or the lack of liability on the part of the insured. If it is determined early on that the insured was in no way responsible for the accident, the insured's company can deny any claim made by the other person(s) involved. The insured then goes to the other driver's insurance company and makes a claim for any physical damage to the vehicle and any bodily injury claim he has.

If there is a question of who may be responsible for the accident, then the adjuster may have to obtain information from all the sources mentioned earlier in this chapter, making a determination of who was at fault.

It's important that an insured answer all of the questions his adjuster asks as comply and correctly as possible – even if the answers are not favorable to the insured. I have taken statements from an insured individual, then received completely different answers to the same questions from other people involved in the accident (and, in consequence, had to return to the insured to "compare notes". Sometimes the insured would remain firm that what she had told me was what had happened, but usually the insured would acknowledge that he had not told me all the facts about the accident.

The privacy restrictions now in place prevent adjusters from getting information from some sources without written consent from the person involved. It's known that the sooner contact is made with an involved party, the more likely the adjuster is going to get an accurate account of what that person remembers.

One such area is ambulance personnel. I have worked accidents where one or more of the persons were transported by ambulance to a hospital. After receiving the assignment, I would go to the ambulance carrier and interview the Emergency Medical Technician, driver and anyone else who was at the scene of the accident. I would ask them if anyone who was transported mentioned anything in particular about details of the accident, and they could tell me if anything was said and what was said. Unfortunately, we can no longer get any medical bills or records from doctors, hospitals or ambulance personnel without a written, signed authorization from the person involved... making the adjuster's job all that more difficult.

Chapter 10

Liability Settlement

Insurance claims that involve liability settlements include **uninsured** motorists – are you familiar with the settlement issues surrounding an uninsured motorist? With today's constant emphasis on proof of insurance, the problem doesn't come up very often, but the questions remain:

📄🖐️   How does an uninsured liability clause protect the insured?

📄🖱️   How is it settled?

📄🗂️   Is the insured responsible for any damage at all?

The adjuster handling a claim for the insured's company has certain information to gather if that claim involves an uninsured driver. Likewise, the insured must be able to give the adjuster as much information as possible – without the right facts, the adjuster may not make the right decision on whether the liability coverage applies to the claim.

Uninsured motorist coverage hinges on two important criteria, both of which must be established before it becomes a part of the Bodily Injury claim filed by the insured:

3. **No insured responsibility.** First, it must be determined that the insured is in no way responsible for the accident that caused the bodily injury to the insured. If the investigation reveals the insured was responsible in any way for the accident – even as a percentage – the coverage does not apply to the accident claim.

4. **Qualifying uninsured.** The adjuster must establish that the other person involved in the accident is totally responsible for the accident, and that person has no liability insurance that covers responsibility for the accident. Only applies to Bodily Injury claim, not to Property Damage claim . Coverage does not apply to the insured vehicle unless the insured has Collision coverage. Then a deductible usually applies to the loss amount to arrive at the claim amount.

Today, most states require that anyone insuring a road-licensed vehicle carry liability insurance. Most states also require that proof of insurance be provided when applying for a driver's license or vehicle license plates. Why do many individuals still drive without any type of insurance coverage? Reasons for lack of insurance include:

- Accident frequency
- Traffic violations
- Suspended license
- Criminal conviction

Tip: It's common practice for a police, highway patrol or sheriff's department accident report to include information

on the insurance carried by the motorists involved – what company (or companies) are providing coverage, and what level of coverage each driver is carrying.

Check your policy to determine the coverage you're carrying for Uninsured Motorists.

Chapter 11

<u>Bodily Injury Settlement</u>

Truly, a topic that's "clear as mud" – I know of no other type of insurance claim that can involve more emotion, opinion and math than an injury claim!

For example, consider an insured motorist that has an accident resulting in injuries to three passengers in the other car (the driver, his wife in the front seat and a daughter in the back seat). The insured is at fault for the accident, and must consider not only the medical attention for the injured, but their car – which is a total loss. And that's not all: don't forget the luggage and personal items in the trunk. How is such a complex claim handled?

The most common method of settling injury claims is that familiar measurement: the dollar. In this case, the questions are:

　　▤▥ How much does the insurance company owe the driver for the three year-old car that was totaled?

　　▤▧ How much does the insurance company owe the driver and two passengers for their injuries? (This can include compensation for medical expenses, lost wages, rehabilitation, pain and suffering and more.)

Naturally, the car will have a Blue Book or NADA Book average value, using the car's age and equipment, so the first figure is easy to calculate. The "human expenses" – medical expenses, lost wages and rehabilitation costs – can be determined by the bills that are submitted for services rendered.

Let's assume that the man and wife had their seat belts on and sustained bruises and cuts in the accident. They're taken to the hospital, checked over, x-rayed and released with a future follow up appointment with their family physician. Let's further assume that the couple was lucky and healed completely, with no impact on their quality of life.

The adjuster needs good communications skills, and must maintain contact with the couple. He'll have to monitor and track their medical bills, and when the couple has recovered, discuss an injury settlement with them. The settlement might involve:

Ambulance bill:	550
Hospital outpatient bill:	1250
Medication:	85
Follow-up visit:	65

	$1,950
Lost wages (2 days off work at $200/day):	400
Bodily injury:	2000

	$4,350

Once the couple agrees to these figures and signs a release, the claim is concluded about 3 weeks after the accident occurred. Note that there is no book that states precisely what the bodily injury compensation should be… this is an intangible figure, a negotiated portion of an otherwise straightforward injury claim.

Companies follow general guidelines for an injury claim, and they usually try to settle the bodily injury portion for one to three times the total of medical expenses and lost wages – this accounts for pain, suffering, emotional distress and so on.

The adjuster maintained good contact and communications with the mother and father until they were ready to talk settlement, and he negotiated the settlement directly with them. The couple also kept their insurance company informed of the development of the claim, and was advised by their insurance company that the offer appeared fair and adequate.

Tip: It's always a good idea to use your own insurance company as a resource, even if you don't call on the company's services.

The daughter sitting in the back seat had quite a different situation – she was 17 years old, beginning her senior year of high school and a starter on her high school basketball team. She didn't have her seat belt fastened, and was sitting behind the driver – since the insured collided with the driver's side of the vehicle, the impact shattered the glass in the rear passenger door. The impact forced the girl into the rear door panel, with her head and face toward the shattered glass. Her injuries consisted of facial lacerations to the left side of her face and neck, two broken ribs, a fractured left wrist and a bruised hip.

Stop for a moment and write down what you think the total claim might be for the injured daughter. (I'll mention that I figured this claim as if the adjuster was able to work with the parents and conclude the claim without the claimants retaining an attorney.) Estimated costs for the daughter included:

5-day Hospital:	7000
Plastic surgeon:	1200
Physical therapy:	4500
Medication:	550
Future plastic surgery to reduce scarring (2 treatments):	10000

	$23,250
Settlement compensation for pain and suffering/emotional distress:	25000

Total settlement for the daughter:	$48,250

A year after the accident, the daughter's wrist and broken ribs healed satisfactorily, and with the help of a good plastic surgeon, the facial scarring was almost unnoticeable. The parents signed a Release and Trust agreement for a total settlement of $48, 250 on the daughter's claims.

The adjuster in this case was thorough, kept in constant contact with the claimants and obtained all the medical information on each claimant (including documentation on medical charges like X-rays, physician's reports and the recovery prognosis on each claimant). The result: a negotiated settlement on all three people to a satisfactory conclusion.

However, the settlement couldn't have been possible without:

    The adjuster understanding what was necessary, and when to act.

    The cooperation and input from the claimants, working with the adjuster.

Sometimes claimants feel the need to retain an attorney to handle claims with the insurance company until a settlement is reached. In most cases, a settlement can be reached between the attorney on behalf of his client and the insurance company, preventing lengthy and costly litigation.

This case also demonstrates the timeliness of updating your insurance coverage! Just five days before the accident I've discussed in this chapter, the insured purchased the car he was driving when the accident occurred. He went to this agent to report the purchase of the car, and asked that it be added to his automobile policy. Before he left the office, the agent asked him to take a few minutes to review his coverage, since it had been a couple of years since the agent had seen the insured.

In reviewing the coverage, it was found that the insured had $25000/$50000 liability coverage on his car, which we know would have been insufficient to cover the total cost of the accident. Had the agent not asked the insured to review the coverage, the insured would not have decided to increase his liability coverage to $50,000/$100000 per accident.

With the increase in coverage limits, the accident was fully covered.

With $25,000/$50,000 limit, daughter's claim payable amount $25,000. Insured had to pay $23,250

Injured	*Per Person (25,000)*	*Total for Accident (50,000)*
Father	4300	4300
Mother	5500	9800
Daughter	48250	25000
Total Amount Not Covered	*23,250*	*n/a (Total less than 50,000)*

With the increased limits: Daughter claim paid in full.

Injured	*Per Person (50,000)*	*Total for Accident (100,000)*
Father	4300	4300
Mother	5500	9800
Daughter	48250	25000
Total Amount Not Covered	*n/a (Each claim covered)*	*n/a (Total less than 100,000)*

Chapter 12

The Flood

What is a flood? A flood as most people think of it, is something that normally is dry becomes covered with water for a period of time. Water accumulates to a depth above normal ground and stays for a period of time. This results in water damage to property.

Some common examples are areas of ground or terrain covered by water in rivers or streams flowing over their banks. Another is the ground or under ground levels of buildings becoming flooded. Basement of homes is an example. Houses built in low lying areas can be flooded by run-off water from excessive rain fall from time to time.

In the early 1970's I lived in Hannibal, Missouri. The Mississippi River went through the east side of Hannibal and was the state dividing line between Missouri and Illinois. In years prior to the early 1970's areas along the river here would become flooded due to high water getting out of the river banks. Since the area on the Hannibal side ran along the east end of the down town district, many buildings got water in them when this happened.

In the early 70's the United States Government created a National Flood Insurance Program. This program was designed to provide an insurance policy especially for properties that were exposed to this type of flooding. This covered large areas that were inundated by flooding conditions resulting in water damaging structures in the flooded area. These areas became known as flood plains and structures qualified to be covered by the flood insurance policy. This was in addition to the regular Homeowners of property policies covering other losses than those caused by flooding.

The first flood I received flood claims on was the flood of 1973. Water got about ten feet above flood stage at the river and flooded area three blocks west from the river and about five blocks north and five blocks south of the middle of down town. Unfortunately for the people, there were not many flood insurance policies in force. By the next flood a few years later, most people in the flood plain had flood insurance on their properties and received money to help with the repair to their properties and damage to contents.

In case this reader wants to inquire about Flood Insurance, most insurance agents do sell this insurance to people who have properties that qualify under the flood policy guidelines.

Adjustment of these claims sometimes were time consuming. In dealing with content items that had been in water, a waiting period often figured in the adjustment time. This was to let the item involved have time to see if it would dry out satisfactorily. Items would dry out but remained stained or discolored. However, the insured wanted to keep the item as a keep-sake or to continue to use it. We would make them a damage allowance. This would usually be a percentage of the value and they keep the item.

Chapter 13

Storm and Catastrophe Adjusting

Many insurance companies have their own staff adjusters who handle only catastrophes and other storms that result in a large volume of claims on one date. Independent **catastrophe adjusting companies** specialize in working storms and catastrophes, such as hurricanes, tornados, hail, floods, explosions, etc., These occurrences generate a large number of claims, sometimes numbering in the thousands, and require many adjusters to get the claims handled as quickly as possible. When the claims have been serviced, the adjusters return to their main office. Adjusters can be gone from four to eight weeks, or longer. Some **independent adjusters** choose to go where the storms occur during the year, and work up to ten months out of the year if the business is available. It is common for a married couple to work storms together, each handling their own share of claims. This enables the couple to make a good living, each bringing in an income. At today's earnings, a couple can make up to $30,000 per storm.

Adjusters go to a storm location, are assigned claims, handle and close them, but do not take these claims back to their office when they are sent home. Any claims not closed are turned over to a "clean up" team for closing.

Chapter 14

Paper to Paperless Communication

What? A Paperless File! Yes!

1. I started handling claims in 1966. At that time electronic communication were limited to telephone, electric typewriters, word processors and telegrams.

2. My first camera used eight-exposure rolls of film. Exposed film had to be taken to a photo lab, and took two days to process. Only then did I have pictures that I could attach to a claim report

3. Claim reports to insurance companies were usually typed (sometimes hand written) and snail-mailed to the insurance company. All statements taken from insureds, claimants, witnesses, etc., were hand-written in the first person. After giving the statement, the person making the statement read the statement and then signed and dated the paper the statement was written on.

4. Damage estimates on damaged property were written in long hand.

5. First class mail at $.03 cents per ounce was the means of getting written information from one place to another.

I retired in 2006 after working forty-two years as a claims adjuster. When I retired most insurance companies were requiring paperless files. Computer technology has revolutionized the insurance industry.

How many of you remember when the idea of sending a man to the moon seemed preposterous?

I had a paperless experience recently when I got my vehicle license plate renewed. I gave the clerk a check for the fee. In less than a minute she returned with a receipt, and returned the check I had just given her in payment. She had scanned the check into the computer, eliminating further need to handle or keep the check in their possession. Paperless transaction!

Chapter 15

Hail Claims

Definition of Hail: Hail stone—A hard pellet of snow and ice that forms hail in the upper atmosphere.

A hailstorm is a storm in which precipitation that falls in the form of hail stones. I will explain more about the varieties of hailstones that can fall in future paragraphs in this chapter. Perhaps you have been in a hailstorm or seen damage to properties that have been damaged by hail. Being in a hailstorm or seen severely damaged property caused by hail are not pleasant experiences.

Hail comes mostly in round or semi-round shapes. It can have smooth or rough surfaces. The size can vary from ¼ inch to baseball size. Hail that has a rough surface and is accompanied by wind usually causes the most extensive damage.

There is also soft hail that usually does not cause damage.

I would like to write about the types of hail damage to various items. I will then explain the most common procedures used by adjusters to work with the insured to reach an agreeable adjustment of the pending claim. Knowing what to expect, the insured will have a good communication with the adjuster and vise-versa during the claim process.

We'll use a hail storm with the following components: Hail two inches in diameter, get a ruler and see how big a two inch hailstone is, rough edges on the stones surface, thirty mile per hour wind, and accumulation of three inches of hail on the ground. This would be a severe storm. Usually the insured will save a number of the stones in their freezer to show the adjuster when the adjuster arrives.

Dwellings can sustain roof, siding, glass, window frames, and trim damage from this storm.

Hail damage to roof surfaces is usually evidenced by a circled indentation in the roofing surface material. The severity of the damage depends on the force the hail hits the roof surface, the age of the roof material, the quality of the roofing material, and the pitch or slope of the roof area. The steeper the slope, the more severe the damage by the impact of the hail to it. Sometimes the impact will be hard enough to go through the roof surface and expose the felt between the roof material and the roof sheathing.

In case of a minor storm, small hail, no wind, no indentations can be found in the roof surface. However, granules may be knocked loose from the roof surface and go down into the gutters. Granule loss is also common with the aging process of the roof material. If the granules in the gutter are the result of the hail hitting them, usually this loss is not covered by insurance. There are some ways the adjuster can explain to the insured that the granules in the gutter after the storm, may have come from the storm, rather that general aging of the roof material.

In a severe storm with wind and large hail, siding is the next part of a structure that can sustain extensive damage. Three types of siding I have dealt with include wood, metal-aluminum, and vinyl. Wood siding usually sustains chipped paint on the surface. If the storm is severe, the siding may be penetrated by the hail stone. Repair if the damage is minor usually consist of sanding the siding, filling the indentations then painting the siding surface. If damage is severe the siding has to be replaced.

Vinyl siding usually sustained cracks or holes in the surface from contact with the hail. This usually necessitates replacement of the siding. Damage usually involves one or two sides of the structure depending on the direction of the hail .

Glass windows, storm doors, and metal frames can be damaged by hail. Restoration usually necessitates replacement of the damaged items.

Automobiles sustain hail damage at times. Usually the exterior panels including fenders, hood, door side panels, rear deck lid and moldings can sustain damage. Back when these panels were made entirely of metal, the repairs consisted of filling the hail dents in the panels with lead, sanding them then refinishing the panels. Today, with many of the panels being made of plastic, if the panel is cracked by the hail, it has to be replaced. Vehicle chrome trim can be damaged and is usually replaced.

There are several settlement options available to the insured and insurance carrier if the repair cost exceeds the market value of the vehicle. This is called a total loss. The insurance company owes the insured the market value less the policy's deductible. The Insurance company takes the car and title, and sells the car for the salvage value agreed on between the company and the salvage buyer.

The insured can elect to keep the vehicle. In this case the insurance company deducts the insured's deductible and the determined salvage value from the agreed settlement figure and leaves the car with the insured.

If the vehicle is repairable, the insured can elect to take the repair figure in payment of the claim, less the policy deductible, and do what he or she wants to with the vehicle.

On ALL settlements, if there is a mortgage on the vehicle, their name will appear on the settlement draft to protect their interest.

It is important that the vehicle owner keep their insurance company up to date on any change in the financial situation of the vehicle. If the loan is paid off, the company releases the title to the insured. If the vehicle is refinanced or used as collateral to borrow money, the insurance company needs to be made aware of this as well in case another claim occurs.

Chapter 16

Summary

As an insured individual, there are a few things to remember that will help prevent problems in the event of a claim:

1. **Check with your agent periodically.** Make sure the limits of your coverage are appropriate for your insured items, because needs and desires change over time.

2. **Maintain adequate liability coverage on your Homeowner's policy.**

3. **Report promptly.** It's important to alert your agent of potential claim situations promptly, especially accidents where other people or properties may become involved.

4. **Keep a record of all your insurance information.** This includes your agent's name, the insurance company and your agent's phone number. I'd recommend a safety deposit box or home fire safe.

5. **Cooperate with your adjuster!** Provide your adjuster with all the information you have relating to the details of your claim.

As an adjuster, or one who is considering becoming an adjuster, ask yourself these questions:

1. **Are you willing to relocate?**

2. **Can you accept the challenge of working with people, especially those under stress?** You must be able to communicate with people, and *listen*.

3. **Are you prepared to study and learn the adjusting procedure?** Be patient with yourself – adjusting is not a business you can learn overnight.

4. **Are you prepared to witness adversity?**

And of course, never forget the most important rule of adjusting:

Insurance adjusting is a rewarding profession and service, responding to the immediate needs of insured individuals and families, claimants, agents and the companies you represent!

My best wishes to you in the future in all your endeavors!

Forms

INSURANCE POLICY INFORMATION SHEET

Home or Building

Insurance Company:

Agent:
Policy Number:
Amount of Policy:
Dwelling:
Contents:
Amount of Deductible:
Policy period:

Building Commercial
Policy Number:
Amount of Building Policy
Amount of Contents Coverage
Co-Insurance
Policy Deductible

Automobile Coverage

Insurance Company:

Agent:
Vehicle #1
Year: Make: Model:

Serial Number:

Coverage: Deductible:
Collision: YES
            NO
Comprehensive: YES
            NO
Liability:
Coverage Limits: Bodily Injury   Property Damage

Your insurance policy will have a Declaration Page with this information on it.

For a second or third vehicle use above worksheet inserting the figures that apply to those vehicles.

About the Author

Beginning in 1965 and for the next forty-two years I worked as a Multi-Line adjuster. I worked for independent adjusting companies for twenty nine years, and owned my own business for thirteen years. Total Career Forty Two years. In sharing this knowledge and experience in these stories I hope the reader will become more comfortable dealing with an adjuster when they are faced with a claim. I reside with my wife in Columbia, Missouri.